Women Authors to Ignite & Inspire

Discover 26 Indie Voices in Fiction, Nonfiction, and Poetry

Women Authors to Ignite & Inspire

Discover 26 Indie Voices in Fiction, Nonfiction, and Poetry

Nicole Fende

CREATOPIA
An Imprint of Tesseray Publishing

*To everyone who believes their
next favorite author is out there,
waiting to be discovered.*

Book and Cover Design: Monette Satterfield

ISBN 978-1-961912-07-6
Published by Creatopia LLC, An Imprint of Tesseray Publishing LLC
7635 148th Street W, #329, Apple Valley, MN 55124
www.Creatopia.Studio

Contents

Introduction

Have you ever experienced the moment when you finish a book which has moved you, inspired you, or kept you turning pages late into the night, and wondered what's next?

You want a new book to read, one that will be as good as the one you just finished. Our instinct is to look at bestseller lists, bookstore endcaps, or who's in the media talking up their latest release. Many people don't realize some of the most compelling voices in contemporary literature aren't showing up in these places. They're independent authors, often women, creating remarkable work without the marketing muscle of major publishing houses behind them.

This book exists to bridge that gap.

Women Authors to Ignite & Inspire serves a dual purpose. It amplifies the voices of twenty-six talented indie women authors who deserve wider recognition, while simultaneously offering readers a curated guide to discovering fresh, authentic voices across fiction, nonfiction, and poetry. These are real women, absolutely no AI generated content here. Consider it your literary GPS to writers you haven't met yet but will be glad you found.

These authors represent the full spectrum of creative expression. There are novelists crafting stories that transport and transform, nonfiction writers illuminating human experience with clarity and insight, business women offering proven advice, and poets distilling complex emotions into language that resonates. Some write from home offices surrounded by beloved books and drowsy cats. Others draw inspiration from water views and forest trails. One author creates amid a backyard menagerie, writing about "smelling the sun and tasting the air" while chickens cluck nearby. They're united by the quality of their work and their commitment to their craft.

Each profile in this collection offers three essential elements: a biographical sketch that introduces you to the person behind the prose, selected quotes that reveal her perspective on writing and creativity, and detailed information about her published works. Whether you're drawn to page-turning fiction, thought-provoking memoir, or verse that captures what we struggle to articulate, you'll find multiple entry points to connect with these authors and their books.

You'll also notice we've included a section on the Twin Cities Women's Choir, and there's a reason for that. These authors don't create in isolation. They're part of a vibrant community of women finding ways to be heard, support one another, and contribute to the cultural landscape around them. The choir represents another powerful form of women's creative expression. They're a reminder, whether through the written word or through song, women are building connections and amplifying each other's voices. It's about community, collaboration, and the many ways women choose to share their gifts with the world.

We believe you'll discover at least one author in these pages whose work speaks directly to you. We hope you'll seek out her books, be moved by her words, and perhaps share your discovery with others searching for their next meaningful read. These writers have already done the challenging work of creating and publishing their books. Now they need what every author needs most, readers who will give their work a chance.

Independent women authors are out there, writing books that matter, stories that need to be told, words that deserve to be read. They're just waiting to be discovered.

Turn the page, and discover your next favorite woman author.

"Turn the page, and discover your next favorite woman author."

✦ Alexis Acker-Halbur ✦

Alexis Acker-Halbur is an international and national book award-winning author, a medical miracle, and completely odd.

Through her writing, Alex helps others find mind, body, spirit healing from traumatic experiences to build healthy and purposeful lives.

https://nevergiveupinstitute.org

Ask the Author

What inspired you to write your latest (or favorite) book? Like the main character in The Bear: In the Middle of Between, I too have grown weary of a world filled with abuse and trauma. Writing is my way to shout out the pain I feel, and eliminate the suffering in my life.

What's one thing readers often don't know about your work? Though my writing is darkly serious, I always offer tools to bring healing to our minds, bodies, and spirits.

What's a favorite line or passage from your book? You are not responsible for your trauma!

Why do you write? Writing is my passion. The ability to write well is a long and difficult process, but a wonderful experience.

What's next for you as an author? More writing!

In three words, describe your writing style. Mysteriously chaotic adventures

Awards

"Writing is my passion."

International Impact Book Award winner [Fiction 2024]

Living Now Gold Medal Book Award: Books for Better Living [Non-Fiction 2014]

The Bear: In the Middle of Between

The story of a young woman who can no longer live in a world of abuse. Claudia Matthew's abuser was not a stranger, a boyfriend, or a husband. He was her father — the one person who should unconditionally protect and love her. Abused by him since age six, Claudia believes "she is bad." Why else was she the only one of five siblings to always be his victim? In her mind, she kept asking, "Why me?" until her nightmares and feelings of being unloved and unworthy prevailed.

www.amazon.com

Never Give Up: Break the Connection Between Stress and Illness

If stress and anger are making you sick, this book can help you find peace and joy in your everyday life or give you the courage to open a new door to a healthy and fulfilling future. Alexis Acker-Halbur offers anyone who has suffered trauma or loss not just one way forward, but many. A survivor herself of abuse, cancer, and a severe car accident, she describes the connection between mind, body, and spirit.

www.amazon.com

T.R.U.T.H. Program: The Road to Unresolved Trauma Healing

One of the first lessons we learn as children is to tell the truth. For children who are physically, emotionally, and psychologically abused and traumatized, this lesson becomes a dire challenge. Frequently threatened and told to lie, these adult children finding themselves ebbing further and further from the truth.

https://nevergiveupinstitute.org

Colleen Baldrica

Inspired by the teachings of her Native American grandmother, Colleen Baldrica began her spiritual journey as a child. Colleen is an official Chippewa (Ojibwe) Tribe Member, of the White Earth Indian Reservation in Northern MN. Colleen holds a Masters degree in School Counseling and a PhD in the Philosophy of Education.

http://treespiritedwoman.com

Ask the Author

What inspired you to write your latest (or favorite) book? I had a reoccurring dream that I had to write this book and when the time was right, I started.

What's one thing readers often don't know about your work? This book was something I knew I had to do and when the words would come, I would write

What's a favorite line or passage from your book? "I will talk mostly to women, as I am a woman, and I know women best. But what I will share will be good for men to know as well. I will tell you what I know to be true, and it will be up to you to pass it on."

Why do you write? I write for fun, I do not need the need to publish again.

What's next for you as an author? Tree Spirited Woman is going to be celebrating its 20th Anniversary and is still selling well. I hope to make this coming year a great marketing year!

In three words, describe your writing style. Simple, Thoughtful, Heartfelt

Awards

2025 Winner International Impact

2014 Silver Living Now Evergreen

2008 Finalist National Indie Excellence

2007 Bronze Annual Independent Publisher

2006 Finalist Best Books 2006

Tree Spirited Woman: A Story of Spiritual Awakening and Life Enrichment

Written as a narrative, Tree Spirited Woman is an intensely inspiring story that will provide each reader with an abundant opportunity to grow alongside the book's main character. Simple philosophies for living flow through each of the chapters. This is a book that can be read and reread, with deeper understanding and personal awakening culled from each visit to its pages.

http://treespiritedwoman.com

"I had a reoccurring dream that I had to write this book"

Excerpt

I first met her while hiking through the woods behind the college. She was old even then. Her face was lined from years of laughter, sun, and wind. Her light-brown eyes held flecks of gold, and I remember thinking she could see deep into my soul. I felt she knew my life and my thoughts. Her smile was very special. It brightened up her face, causing her eyes to sparkle. It was the moment I first saw that smile that I felt she could be trusted totally. Our unique relationship had begun.

I was in my third year of college and I loved to hike in the woods behind the school, especially in the fall. The leaves seemed to shout out. Their colors were so loud and glorious. Whenever I walked the woods, I felt at peace.

This particular fall day, while hiking deep in the woods...

✦ Katherine Barton ✦

Katherine Barton's work focuses on facing life's most difficult challenges with humor, acceptance and authenticity. She practices a spiritual path

https://kabarton.com

Ask the Author

What inspired you to write your latest (or favorite) book? I wrote it because I had felt trapped in my marriage and was scared to leave it. I wanted people to know that they could leave situations that were not life giving to them and that they would thrive, even though it wasn't easy.

What's one thing readers often don't know about your work? It is compassionate, authentic and funny. I think life is hilarious and gets better the more you have compassion for yourself and others.

Awards

Yearning for Love received a starred review from Kirkus Reviews.

What's a favorite line or passage from your book? Healing has a rhythm as complex and enigmatic as a Beethoven symphony. Some days it beats softly, other days it knocks you over like a sudden wave at the beach.

Why do you write? To understand myself and go deeper with my life and to inspire others with what I find out.

In three words, describe your writing style. Humorous, spiritual, memoir

Yearning for Love: A Reluctant Divorcee's Rocky Road to Nirvana

An aging mom realizes with shock and sorrow she cannot remain in her marriage. Bereft with grief, she fights against her new status at every point, confronting car mechanics and innocent bystanders with her tearful woes. Her teenage daughter's angry response and her own inner turmoil add to the emotional fallout.

https://bookshop.org

"Healing has a rhythm as complex and enigmatic as a Beethoven symphony."

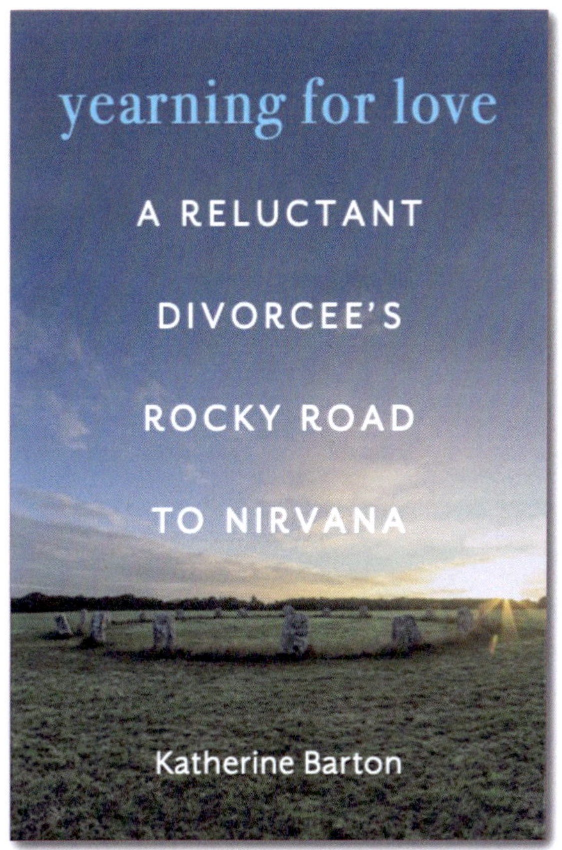

Excerpt

I turned to my friend and said, "I'm Rosie the Riveter of codependence."

She smiled, dragging her fingers in the water. "You aren't alone."

Sighing, I draped my legs over the gunwales into the coolness of the lake. Just weeks after our marriage ended, I could see how deeply I had participated in destroying the vessel that held us which was nowhere near as sturdy as this canoe. Gratefully, I was equally blessed with an acorn seed of divinity and a deep knowing that things were going to be all right over the long run.

Even with that prescient knowledge, I knew that the pathway ahead contained hidden traps. Yet I held a portion of faith that pulled me along the journey, giving me uncanny and unexpected endurance. Off I went, naked, vulnerable, and whimpering. It would be years before I would be able to understand how deeply. Ihad chosen to be a victim, costing me years as I avoided my own strength and agency. Like a panicked stallion, I was paralyzed in quicksand and had only a bare sense of hope to go forward. It would have to be enough.

✦ Leanne M. Benson ✦

Through the window of Leanne M Benson's modest art studio, the hardwood forest opens to a spring-fed trout stream that meanders into the distance. This magical place inspires each of her lyrical words and brushstrokes to play a part in whisking both children and adults into a wonderful adventure.

www.leannembenson.com

Ask the Author

What inspired you to write your latest (or favorite) book? I enjoy watching the excitement and fascination grow in a child's eyes as I read stories to classrooms throughout Minnesota. If Off the Wall World Tours! inspires just one child to learn more about the world, then it's well worth every minute and dime I've spent creating this children's book!

What's a favorite line or passage from your book? If you'd like to go places, but think that you couldn't,

Do the wacky things they say, "You mustn't!", or "You shouldn't!"

Just open a book about whimsical things

And fly through the pages, as if they were wings. ~from Off the Wall World Tours!

Why do you write? As long as I can remember, I've loved to create things. I love to paint magical things that could never be captured with a camera. I enjoy putting words together in unconventional ways. My husband razzes me, "You can't ever 'Not create'!"

What's next for you as an author? I'll be creating twenty-eight more 16x20 oil painted illustrations to go along with my crazy lyrics for the second and third Off the Wall World Tours! books. These stories will take readers in and around Europe, Africa, Middle East, Asia, and Oceania.

In three words, describe your writing style. Playful, Lyrical, Unconventional

" Being an author, illustrator, and storyteller is more a passion of mine than a job."

The Unbelievable Topsy Turvy Day!

This humorous story is capturing the curiosity of youngsters everywhere. And its whimsical illustrations are turning heads of all ages as it begs to be turned upside-down ...or is it upside-right?

www.leannembenson.com

The Lion of Tupungato

This story takes you on a historic fictional journey. A young girl learns of her great-grandmother's struggles, and how through an amazing friendship with a lion, she is saved.

www.leannembenson.com/

Jennifer Bierma

Jennifer has been utilizing her gifts as an intuitive healer to assist clients since the age of nineteen. It is her hope that this book, and the lessons she has learned about fear, acceptance, love and social norms, will help others step into their gifts and live life more authentically.

www.rejennerationwellness.com

Ask the Author

What inspired you to write your latest (or favorite) book? This book was written as a journal of my memories. After I began to write it, spirit jumped in and it turned into something much more than that. It turned into the biggest moment of healing in my life.

What's one thing readers often don't know about your work? This was the story of my beginnings. This is far from the end of my learning journey and there are many things in the book that I have learned far more about since that time.

In three words, describe your writing style. Conversational, Experiential, Evocative

What's a favorite line or passage from your book? "As we look into the empty spaces within us, we often find new life that we did not know was there."

Why do you write? I love the art of story telling and I also love teaching. People can be inspired, their minds opened to new perspectives and their lives prepared for new experiences with just the right combination of words. I experience this for myself when I write and then, I get the opportunity to experience it again through the readers that reach out to me after they have read my book.

What's next for you as an author? I have several children's books in process and a follow up to this book.

"This book...turned into the biggest moment of healing in my life."

A Life Lived Medium: A Psychic's
Journey from Fearful to Almost Fearless

Jennifer can see dead people, but in the
beginning, she didn't know they were
beyond the veil. As a child, she couldn't
explain the people who visited her at night,
the little boy who hid her schoolwork, or the
way she knew of her uncle's death before
her family had even received the news.

Even though she often hid her gifts, the
spirits rarely hid themselves from her. They
continued to tell her about themselves, and
through the process, taught her more
about herself. Eventually, Jennifer came to
realize that her abilities as a
medium—seeing into other dimensions,
conversing with spirits, sensing traumatic
events, and feeling the state of someone's
health--were not something to be feared.

https://spiritandherb.etsy.com

Excerpt

I saw it in a dream, or I suppose you could call it a vision. A beautiful, blond-haired, blue-
eyed boy, about five or six years old, stood over my bed, fighting back tears as he told me
how sad he was that he hadn't been born yet. "When do I get to come see you again?" He
was right there; he was always right there. I reached out to touch him on the cheek. I
could hear the emotion in his voice. He was distraught, and I was worried about him. In
this moment, he felt much more human than ever before. I felt the tug of the blanket as
he tried to wake me up, the texture of his soft skin as he touched my hand, and his breath
on my cheek as he whispered in my ear. I was twenty-two at the time, and he had been
with me as long as I could remember. When I was a child, I didn't understand his
presence. He was comforting at times but scary at others. He would appear out of
nowhere in my dark room and stand over my bed. He would get angry and yell at me when
I didn't listen or I didn't understand something he said. Other times, he would linger in the
background to give me a giant smile of support when I was in trouble or pushing through
my comfort zone to try something new. His presence was confusing to me.

✦ Mary K Crawford-Lorfink ✦

Mary K Crawford-Lorfink graduated from the University of Minnesota with a BA in English and has been published in WINK: Writers in the Know, Creatopia magazine, and Amazon books. She is an ongoing student at The Loft Literary Center in Minneapolis, MN, and a member of WOW – Women of Words. "Writing is a mystical experience – turning wonder into story."

https://marykaycrawfordlorfink.substack

Ask the Author

Why do you write? About ten years ago, I wandered into a Beginner's Creative Writing class in downtown Minneapolis—and boom! Sparks flew. Not the romantic kind, but the creative kind that light a fire under your writing dreams. And here's the best part: I didn't just leave with a notebook full of ideas, I left with friends. Real friends. Laura, Phyllis and I started meeting every few weeks to share our writing, but what we really shared were our lives. Our stories held emotions, milestones, and hard-won truths. Writing them down felt liberating, speaking them aloud, even more so.

Yes, the stories were powerful, but what I treasured most were the conversations that followed—spaces where creativity felt limitless, where encouragement, sensitivity, and generosity of spirit set the tone.

Fast forward a decade, and that spark has turned into three published books, with a fourth on the way. This one is extra special—a WWII story based on my friend Anna's mother, Maria, who was taken by the Nazis from her Ukrainian village to work as forced labor on a German farm. Her resilience and grace continue to inspire me, reminding me why I write in the first place: to honor stories that deserve to be remembered.

What's next for you as an author? Looking forward to completing the book I am currently working on.

In three words, describe your writing style. Hope, peace, love.

Thirteen Diamond Lake Point: A Spirited Mystery

Janet is hired as a personal assistant to Hollywood's daughter, Ava Fleming. Ava is enmeshed in the extravagant lifestyle of an eccentric heiress living somewhat reclusively on a semi-hidden stretch of Diamond Lake. Alone, during an overnight housesitting stay, Janet experiences the eerie feel of a restless presence and is drawn into communion with the spirit world. What do the spirits want from Janet? She allows her instincts to guide her through Ava's strange new world of privilege and need.

www.amazon.com

"For me, writing is a journey of the soul—part peace, part longing, always leading me back to a deeper purpose."

PASSING THROUGH: A Poetic Journey: Spirited Stories and Mysteries

Poetry is everywhere — around us and within us. It flows, cycles, and connects us to all of existence.

It is divination through words, offering images, visions, and introspection of what it takes to be human from beginning to end.

As we celebrate and lament the passing of seasons, it is the journey itself that defines us. There is a quiet peace in knowing that life will not leave us unchanged.

www.amazon.com

Donna M. Cramer

Donna M. Cramer is a retired special education teacher from Massachusetts who spent over 20 years working with young children with special needs. After a brain injury changed her life, she found healing through writing. Today, she writes, practices yoga, and embraces hope with her husband and two Maine Coon cats.

www.authordonnamcramer.com

Ask the Author

What inspired you to write your latest (or favorite) book? The inspiration for this novel came from real life. My husband and I enjoy visiting Las Vegas and usually take a trip there once a year. One evening, while browsing an online magazine for new sights or attractions we might explore, I stumbled across an article about the alarmingly high suicide rate in Las Vegas. It explained that many people choose Las Vegas as a place to die, in part to spare their families the trauma of discovering them.

What's one thing readers often don't know about your work? I don't spend hours, days, or weeks meditating or praying for inspiration—it simply appears. Sometimes I hear a snippet of dialogue in my head, jot it down, and build a story from there.

Why do you write? I was a teacher for many years until my brain injury. A speech therapist suggested I try writing. So my dream sprang into being.

What's a favorite line or passage from your book? "Could it be possible for us to choose hope over despair?"

What's next for you as an author? Today, I have a series of three children's books about Lester Lion published by Kirk House Publishers. My debut adult novel, Paul Is Missing, is out now, and I'm currently working on my second, Vegas Goodbye.

In three words, describe your writing style. Resilient. Compassionate. Hopeful.

"I often carry characters around in my mind for months, slowly developing their personalities and voices."

Vegas Goodbye

Amid the glitz and ache of Las Vegas, two broken souls collide in a story of grief, connection, and redemption. Debra, a widow stranded in sorrow, can't move beyond her husband's death. John, a father gutted by his son's overdose, is haunted by guilt he cannot outrun. Both arrive in Vegas with the same devastating purpose—to end their lives in a city long notorious for despair. A chance encounter sparks an unexpected bond, even as each hides the worst of their pain. Then Jim appears: a menacing figure who stalks John's steps. Is he real, or the dark echo of trauma made flesh? As Debra and John draw closer, they must face their pasts, their guilt, and the shadow that won't let them go. In the city of illusions, Vegas Goodbye becomes a testament to fragile grace—the flicker that proves even at the edge, a new beginning can still ignite.

www.kirkhousepublishers.com/donnamcramer

Paul is Missing

Two young families stand on the cusp of new beginnings. Brynn and Eric Branson, newly married, are overjoyed with their baby, Paul. Alison and Jared Jensen are equally thrilled to start their life together, and Alison longs to escape the grip of her overbearing father, Cecil. But when Jared is deployed to Afghanistan, everything tilts.

www.kirkhousepublishers.com/donnamcramer

Lester Lion Loses Grandpa

Lester Lion Loses Grandpa is a tender, compassionate picture book that helps young children understand the big feelings that follow losing someone they love. When Lester's dad picks him up from school with sad, shiny eyes, Lester learns his beloved Grandpa has died.

www.kirkhousepublishers.com/donnamcramer

✦ Katelyn Davida Mariah ✦

Katelyn is a visionary Artist who has shown her work internationally. She is an award-winning author of 9 books on various subjects focused on empowering adults and child. Katelyn is also a traditionally trained herbalist. The books she has authored has enabled her to combine all three of her passions

https://mystickcreekpublishing.com

Ask the Author

What inspired you to write your latest (or favorite) book? My Latest book, Sacred Botanicals was inspired by the question "I wonder if ancient goddess cultures worked with herbs?" I was surprised what I found went I started to do the research. There was so much that I didn't know that intrigued me.

Once I decided that it would make an informative book, inspiration started to flow magically.

Awards

Winner of the 2015 National Indie Excellence Award for Alternative Medicine

Winner of the 2016 Best Book Award Finalist in Health:Alternative Medicine

What's one thing readers often don't know about your work? It is that it is highly intuitive and I am inspired through a higher connection in myself. The writing in my newest book is a combination of visionary storytelling and research.

What's next for you as an author? I just finished Sacred Botanicals, there is marketing and promotion and I am creating a new line of herbal products to go with it. There will be 13 products to go with each of the 13 goddesses in the book.

In three words, describe your writing style. Magical, creative, visionary

"It all came together in a fun, magical, multi sensory learning experience."

Sacred Botanicals: Remembering the Herbal Ways of the Ancient Feminine

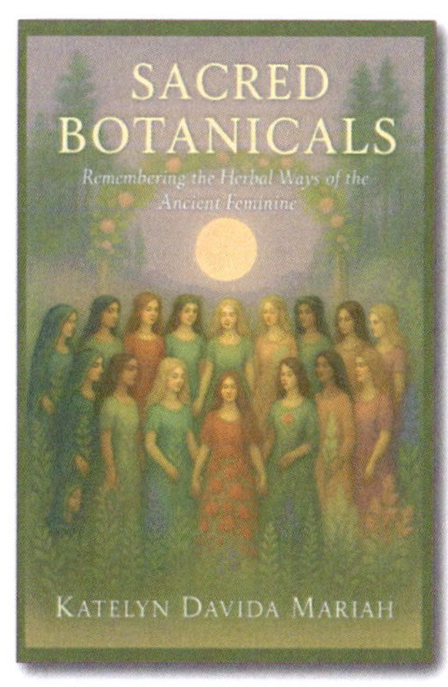

I have found that working with the plants is not only about physical healing, but also energy, frequency, and spirit. As I studied herbalism, I felt drawn to the traditions of those that came before. The goddesses the and priestesses who tended the ancient sacred gardens. I realize now that their wisdom was not lost but it was waiting to be remembered and reclaimed.

https://mystickcreekpublishing.com

Empowered Health and Wellness: Awakening the Inner Physician

Katelyn has worked with her inner physician for 35 years. She feels it is one of the most important relationships. The inner physician has guided her through some very serious physical issues with grace and ease. It's a health and wellness laboratory in a book.

https://mystickcreekpublishing.com

Magic of Alchemy Journal: Personal journal for herbal studies

Magic of Alchemy: a unique personal journal for herbal studies. Immerse yourself in the enchanting realm of herbal wisdom as this comprehensive guide unveils the medicine behind each herb, offering a journey of self-discovery and holistic well-being. Whether you're a novice or an experienced herbalist, unlock the transformative power of nature with this captivating exploration of the magical art of alchemy.

https://mystickcreekpublishing.com

Andrea Easton

Andrea Easton has a master's in Clinical Mental Health counseling. After 12 years of marriage, she suddenly became a widow. In 2009, the love of her life succumbed to cancer, a short 10 weeks after his diagnosis of a type of cancer caused by Agent Orange. Devastated, Andrea discovered how hurtful the loss of her "big love" impacted other parts of her life, as well as her heart. Her personal journey became her inspiration to help others recover from loss and dark times.

https://thenewnormaltlg.wordpress.com

Ask the Author

What inspired you to write your latest (or favorite) book? Processing my own grief and all the oddities around it. People see you as the same because physically on the outside you look the same, yet inside you are a mess.

What's one thing readers often don't know about your work? That is has helped people in not only the grief of a person. It has helped leave an abusive relationship and realizing things about their marriages. This wasn't something I expected. Yet so amazing!

What's a favorite line or passage from your book? Grief is not linear, more like a rollercoaster; ups and downs are so much a part of the grieving process. Nothing about grieving is the same for anyone, nor does it follow the same patterns.

Why do you write? I find it cathartic.

What's next for you as an author? I have three books started and just came up with a new idea for a book, which is going to be my next work.

In three words, describe your writing style. Honest, warm, compelling

" People see you as the same because physically on the outside you look the same, yet inside you are a mess."

The New Normal®: The Life of Grief

A refreshingly honest discussion of one person's grief journey from the onset of grief at the point of the terminal diagnosis of her loved one, to the present time. She takes you through pain, loss and suffering, as well as day-to-day challenges, personally and socially, and many varied efforts to navigate the new world of a dramatic identity change.

https://thenewnormaltlg.wordpress.com

The New Normal ®: Journaling Grief

A journal that helps you understand the areas of grief that are holding you back. There are many factors to the healing process and while not easy to work through - working through is the only way to relieve the feelings.

https://thenewnormaltlg.wordpress.com

Nicole Fende

Nicole Fende, A.S.A, an experienced Chief Financial Officer, former investment banker, and credentialed actuary, left the corporate world to become The Numbers Whisper®, and focus on helping creative business owners prosper. She publishes books and board games through Tesseray Publishing, is Co-Founder of Creatopia.

www.TesserayPublishing.com

Ask the Author

What inspired you to write your latest (or favorite) book? I was looking for a memorable, fun way to help my clients learn small business skills. I realized I needed my own world, and stories. Ones that I owned. I've been reading and writing science fiction since I was a kid. It was a natural progression to create my alter ego, Bounty Hunter Brenna Rain, and create an adventure for her with The Prosperity Dimension.

What's one thing readers often don't know about your work? My books have inspired board games. Two are in development, while the anthology is directly tied to a published game called Body Be Gone.

In three words, describe your writing style. Engaging, uninhibited, fun

Why do you write? I've been making up stories my entire life. I love imagining a world, and then sharing it with others to experience and enjoy.

What's next for you as an author? I'm working on a Sci-Fi Romance set in the same universe as The Prosperity Dimension.

What's a favorite line or passage from your book? "Look," she said keeping her voice low, "do you want me to save my badassery for the bad guys, or give you a personal demonstration right now?" – Brenna Rain in The Prosperity Dimension

"I love imagining a world, and then sharing it with others to experience and enjoy."

The Prosperity Dimension: A Small Biz Sci-Fi Adventure

Join Brenna Rain, bounty hunter and starship captain, as she navigates a deadly job gone wrong. With a mysterious client and assassins on her trail, she must use every skill to survive and secure her profit.

This groundbreaking graphic novel combines pulse-pounding sci-fi with practical small business wisdom.

www.amazon.com

How to be a Finance Rock Star: The Small Business Owner's Ticket to Multi-Platinum Profits

You started your business to make money, but trying to build profits without understanding finance is like a rock band performing without electric guitars. It falls flat.

This entertaining, easy-to-understand guide gives entrepreneurs the financial knowledge they need to succeed. Learn to overcome your fear of numbers, discover how just four key metrics drive profitability, and avoid the profit black holes that trap many business owners.

www.amazon.com

Body Be Gone Origins Unearthed: An Anthology of Tales from the Start of the World's Premiere Corpse Removal Service

Mopping Up Loose Ends Since 1927.

The new owners of Body Be Gone™, the premier body disposal business in the world, are trying to uncover the lost history of the franchise. We know the business started in 1927, but we don't know where or how.

www.bodybegone.com

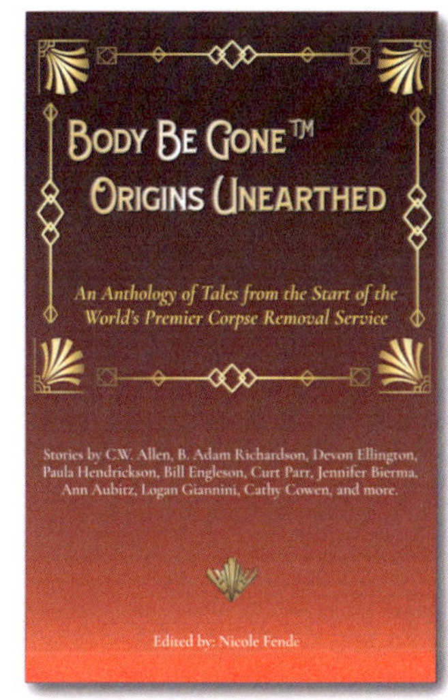

Amy Gleason

Amy Gleason is a novelist of the Woodland Hills teen fiction series, as well as the author & illustrator of two children's books. She lives with her husband and two daughters in Stillwater, Minnesota, where she finds tremendous inspiration for her stories. She is always writing, but also enjoys running, biking, teaching, scrapbooking, and traveling.

www.amygleason.net

Ask the Author

What inspired you to write your latest (or favorite) book? How about what inspired me to write my FIRST "novel"? When I was in 5th grade, I watched a rerun episode of the old tv sitcom I Love Lucy (1954), where Lucy suddenly decides she's going to write a novel. The day I saw that episode was the day I decided I wanted to be a novelist! I wrote my first "novel" the next week, when I drafted a 31 page hand-written story for my weekly essay assignment at school. After that, there was no stopping me!

What's one thing readers often don't know about your work? For my novels, it all began in December of 1984, when my mom made me a homemade Cabbage Patch Kid doll for Christmas. I named her Joanna (because the materials to make the doll all came from the craft store, JoAnn Fabrics), and I created a whole world around her.

What's next for you as an author? My novel series is where my passion is, and I have at least the next four or five books already outlined.

Why do you write? I see so many inspiring situations going on around me, many of which become the 'spark' of my next storyline. I don't always like how things transpire in real life, but through writing, I get to decide the outcome.

" I see so many inspiring situations going on around me, many of which become the 'spark' of my next storyline"

Penguin's Journey Home

Penguin doesn't like living in the cold. But is there a better place for him to live? Follow along on this colorful journey, as this little lost penguin finds his way home!

https://store.bookbaby.com/book/penguins-journey-home

After Tomorrow

When Joanna's relationships with members of the opposite sex start going in new directions all at once, she finds herself struggling with contradictions between the messages of society and her own personal value system.

After Tomorrow takes you through those riveting days of high school drama in the mid-1990s, long before cell phones, text messaging, and widespread social media. Joanna embraces these challenges, one day at a time in her humble life, as she prepares for all that lies ahead.

https://store.bookbaby.com/book/after-tomorrow

Timber Hall

The first year of college at UW-Timberwood presents a whole new life for Joanna Conors. Here she meets Avrie Daniels, the greatest roomie ever, and the girls immediately become best friends. Their adjustment to living in a dorm, juggling a full course load, and figuring out the college social scene is challenging, but the Roomies embrace this journey together with enthusiasm and flair.

https://store.bookbaby.com/book/timber-hall

Barb Greenberg

Barb Greenberg, an award-winning author, writes books that remind women of their courage, strength, and the power of their voices. With a background in English education and a lifelong love of stories, her encouraging, comforting, humorous, and thought-provoking books inspire readers. A Minnesota native, she now enjoys life in New Mexico.

www.authorbarbgreenberg.com

Ask the Author

What inspired you to write your latest (or favorite) book? I wrote Rose Hope to remind women they are not alone, not only during divorce, but during any difficult life transition, and to remember to trust their intuition and their strength.

What's one thing readers often don't know about your work? I write on a yellow legal pad. I know that dates me! There are days the words just flow and days when the faucet turns off, but I write anyway, just in case something appears.

Awards

GOLD medal winner of the 31st Annual Midwest Book Awards

What's a favorite line or passage from your book? "I might not be hot stuff anymore, but I'm still stuff and some of my stuff, though possibly lukewarm, is still pretty darn good."

Why do you write? Writing helps me be braver. Well, until my first book signing, when I realized people were going to actually read what I wrote. Yikes!

What's next for you as an author? Cheering on my book as it makes its way into the world.

In three words, describe your writing style. Conversation with friends.

"Writing helps me be braver. Well, until my first book signing, when I realized people were going to actually read what I wrote. Yikes!"

Rose Hope

RSVPing yes to a bridal shower in the midst of her own divorce is not one of the better decisions Rosie has made, but she's been distracted. She's discovered that being a "nice" girl is not all it's cracked up to be. Plus, struggling to keep from disappearing and determined to hold onto her dream has been much harder than Rosie expected, and she's not sure she's up to it. Heartfelt storytelling explores her confusion, self-doubt, fear, and grief with deep emotional insights and touches of humor. We can't help but cheer Rosie on, realizing that in whatever circumstances we may find ourselves, there is always the blossoming promise of a new beginning.

www.kirkhousepublishers.com/barbgreenberg

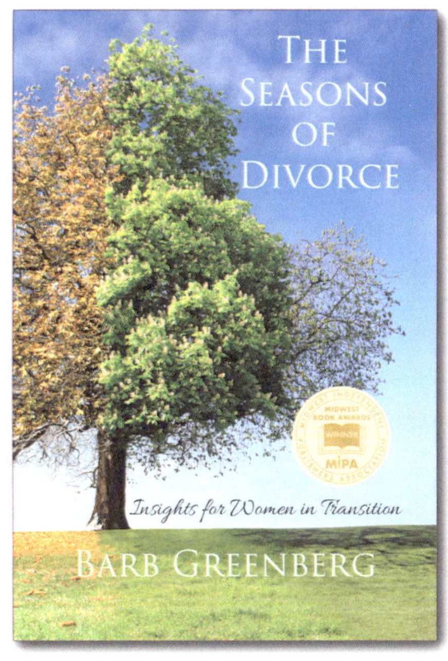

The Seasons of Divorce: Insights for Women in Transition

Wherever you are in the divorce process, The Seasons of Divorce offers support for your journey, and reminds you that you are braver than you ever imagined—and that you are not alone.

If you are feeling lost, it offers direction. If you are grieving, it offers healing and compassion. if you despair about anything wonderful coming out of your pain, it offers hope.

The journey through divorce can be a difficult and often painful, yet it offers an extraordinary gift: the gift of rediscovering yourself.

www.kirkhousepublishers.com/barbgreenberg

✦ Carolyn Hawkins ✦

A native Floridian, Carolyn enjoys watching sunrises and sunsets, listening to the varied sounds of nature, and pondering the latest interesting thing. She enjoys sharing her discoveries with others in hope that it brings a bit of joy to their lives.

www.amazon.com

Ask the Author

What inspired you to write your latest (or favorite) book? I wrote "The Advent Journal for Busy Women" to encourage people to take time for themselves as they journey through the last month of the year and prepare for the next one.

What's one thing readers often don't know about your work? My cats are my co-authors.

What's a favorite line or passage from your book? Peace and joy to you as you move toward the new year and a new you!

Why do you write? To share discoveries I think will be helpful to others.

What's next for you as an author? I have a few ideas in mind.

In three words, describe your writing style. Driven by curiosity.

"My cats are my co-authors."

The Advent Journal for Busy
Women: A Guided Journal for
Stress Relief, Memory Keeping and
Creativity in the Holiday Season

I want to help you experience the best of
this season. This series of words is
designed to help you take a moment to
think about where you are and where you
want to be. It is intended to give you a way
to enjoy a peaceful time just for you.

https://creatopia.studio/shop/stationery-
papercraft/journals-notebooks/the-advent-
journal-for-busy-women/

Sample Prompt

Anticipation

What makes your heart flutter with anticipation?

Are you more likely to stock up on food or hobby supplies in anticipation of stormy
weather?

Which season do you wait for with a sense of anticipation?

C. Kelly

C. Kelly remembers buying an armful of romance novels from her local library in junior high. She fell in love with happily ever afters and is thrilled to be bringing her own happily ever after stories to life. When she's not writing, she loves spending time with family.

www.authorckelly.com/

Ask the Author

What inspired you to write your latest (or favorite) book? This book was inspired by the idea of writing a romance about a reality TV show that didn't include women fighting over a guy.

What's one thing readers often don't know about your work? I often hear the characters speaking to each other in my head. So much of my dialogue is just me writing down what they said. I think this is the one time it's okay to hear voices in my head.

Why do you write? Writing is my way of reminding people of the goodness and kindness in the world. Most people are good and I love showcasing that in my stories.

I also write romance because I think love, in all of its forms, is vital in our world. In the end nothing matters more than love.

What's next for you as an author? I'm writing a romance about a fairy grandmother, think godmother with grey hair and a bit of flair; a twisted ankle; and a killer on the loose.

In three words, describe your writing style. Engaging, Dialogue-driven

Awards

Midwest Independent Publisher's Award, Silver Finalist

"In the end nothing matters more than love."

Thrown by Love

Carrie Nelson applies to be on a reality show to learn how to become a bull rider and ranch hand to help her family pay for an experimental medical treatment for her sister. The work proves to be physically demanding and dangerous; however, it's the ranch owner, Joel Roulston, who is the one thing she could never have anticipated. While experiencing the unexpected ride, will Carrie allow herself to be thrown into love?

www.amazon.com

Excerpt

"What happened?"

"You got thrown from that stupid bull. You must be the unluckiest person on the face of this planet. No one gets thrown from that bull," Joel thundered.

"Oh. Guess I should have realized that," Carrie quietly responded

All of the air left Joel's lungs. He was taking out his fear on her, and even he knew that wasn't fair. "How do you feel?" he asked in a gentler tone of voice.

"Stupid?"

He wasn't sure how she could make him smile when only just a few moments ago he had been scared out of his mind and unable to breathe for worry over her. "How else do you feel?"

"Am I supposed to be feeling anything other than stupid? How about incompetent? Like a failure? Are any of those the . . . the right answer?" Her voice became softer and softer as she spoke, and Joel almost missed the last few words.

"Carrie, how is your head?"

"Okay."

"Are you in any pain?"

"Umm, I'm not sure."

"Why's that?"

"It's hard to think over the buzzing noise in my head. Can you give me a minute before you ask me anything else?"

Joel stood up and looked to the door. He saw Bull and Drake both standing there with looks of worry on their faces, which reflected what was in Joel's heart. Joel turned back around to Carrie. "I'll wait and let the doctor ask his questions."

✦ Stacey Larsen, Ed.D. ✦

Stacey Larsen, Ed.D. is a Minneapolis-based leadership coach, educator, and consultant. She and her team at Authentic Edge LLC work with senior leaders and organizations to build sustainable habits that strengthen trust, accountability, and culture and support leaders in leading with confidence and connection.

https://AuthenticEdge.com

Ask the Author

What inspired you to write your latest (or favorite) book? I was tired of seeing leaders blamed, labeled as toxic, or handed long lists of competencies they were somehow supposed to master. Smart, responsible leaders told me they felt burned out, frustrated, and weighed down by leadership. I wanted to start a different conversation.

Why do you write? I write because I love leaders. Every day I see them carrying heavy burdens, frustrated by people and situations that feel impossible, and questioning if they are cut out for this. Writing is how I sit beside them and say: you are not broken, and you don't have to do it all yourself.

What's a favorite line or passage from your book? "A good dance doesn't require perfection. If the partners are confident and connected, the mistakes go unnoticed. What people remember is the dynamic."

What's next for you as an author? I'm working on a tip book about the "dance partners" who throw leaders off. Archetypes like Negative Ned or Always Late Allie. My goal is not to villainize them, but to help leaders laugh, unhook from their reactions, and find new ways to dance with even the most difficult personalities.

What's one thing readers often don't know about your work? I don't have all the answers. I write like we're sitting across the table, having a conversation.

In three words, describe your writing style. Honest. Relatable. Thought-provoking.

Reframing the Leadership Dance: The Secret to Finding Your Rhythm as a People Leader

Leaders today are overwhelmed by expectations: motivate, delegate, give feedback, manage change, resolve conflict, stay calm, build relationships, develop people. The list never ends. It is no wonder so many leaders feel tired and weighed down by the burden of doing it all.

In Reframing the Leadership Dance, Stacey Larsen, Ed.D., offers an alternative. Drawing on 25 years as a teacher, coach, and consultant, she introduces the Authentic Edge Leadership Framework, a four-step process that helps leaders move beyond chaos and exhaustion.

At its core, leadership is not a solo performance but a partner dance. This book shows leaders how to hold the frame, set a rhythm, and invite others to shine. Through practical habits, reflective questions, and relatable stories, Stacey helps leaders see that success is not about doing more but about dancing differently, with less stress, more confidence, and stronger connections.

www.amazon.com

"Not about doing more, but about dancing differently."

Dominique Miller

Dominique Miller is a Dutch-American, Minnesota-based poet and illustrator, who creatively expresses herself through words and imaging. She is inspired by her experiences in life, love, cultures and human connection with the natural world. Dominique's poems have appeared in magazines—print and online—and have been included at local art-exhibitions.

www.dominiquemiller.com

Ask the Author

What inspired you to write your latest (or favorite) book? I'm a first-generation Dutch immigrant and for the last decade I have explored new territory—the Midwestern region of the United States. Its beautiful ecosystem became my muse for writing. Nature promotes healing; its therapeutic environment brings me to a peaceful state of mind and the outdoors is filled with writing inspiration for those who listen, touch, smell and observe.

Why do you write? Writing works for me like a bandage as well as an alternative medicine: "It heals wounds and protects cherished moments in life."

What's a favorite line or passage from your book? My favorite passage in OUTSIDE(R) is the first paragraph of my poem Whirlwind:

Unwritten words
keep a page blank.
Unspoken words
dry out the tongue.

What's next for you as an author? The topic for my new book of poetry is: "In search of forgotten dreams in the complexity of adulthood."

In three words, describe your writing style. Authentic, minimalistic, and thoughtful.

"The poems included in "OUTSIDE(R)" and "My Thoughts in a Bundle" would never have been published without the presence of Nature."

OUTSIDE(R): Poems and a Poet at One with Nature

An ode to the natural world, OUTSIDE(R) is filled with poetry that is raw and minimalistic. Miller weaves imaginary words through her observations of nature, expressing life experiences and self-reflective contemplations to evoke memories and emotions.

The reader of these poems will hold up a metaphoric mirror, seeing themselves reflected in sentiments that feel familiar and timeless. The themes of six sections express the cycles of nature and the ebb and flow of the inner human experience.

www.amazon.com

My Thoughts in a Bundle: Poetry in Relationship with Myself, Others, and Nature

We are all part of Nature

We are all part of Creating

My thoughts became written words that formed the sentences bundled in this book. Poetry in a simple and pure way to express my love for Nature. These poems encourage one to embrace the beauty of nature, find the beauty within yourself, and to share this with others. I am sharing this with you through this collection of words & photography in "My Thoughts in a Bundle" … a chapter in my Life.

www.dominiquemiller.com

✦ Terri Morrison Kaiser ✦

Born and raised in northern Wisconsin, she is now a Minnesotan with her heart firmly straddling the state line. When not writing, she enjoys gardening, cooking, traveling, hanging with family, and, most of all, pestering her two sons.

www.terrimorrisonkaiser.com

Ask the Author

What inspired you to write your latest (or favorite) book? The Witness Tree is truly the book of my heart. Helen and Esther are strong women, both of them based on my grandmothers, who were the greatest influences in my life. While the story is pure fiction, their presence flows through my two heroines like a hurricane.

Why do you write? Because these characters won't leave me alone until I get them down on paper!

What's one thing readers often don't know about your work? I am a huge history buff. What in hindsight looks to be simpler times is anything but when digging into research.

What's a favorite line or passage from your book? Helen's long-lost love comes back into her life and tells her he would never hurt her again. Helen's response is, "Yes, you will. You're going to die. We're old. That's the way it is."

What's next for you as an author? I just finished a historical fiction novel titled Wildflowers and a compilation of essays titled Letters from Musky Falls.

In three words, describe your writing style. dramatic, spicy, humorous

" I've come to realize I need to write a romance every once in a while to stretch my funny bone."

Awards
Reader's Favorite Five-Star Book

The Witness Tree

When a skeletal foot slips from the confines of a hollow tree on the Foley farm, Helen Foley is desperate to keep family secrets from spilling forth. But Helen doesn't know everything, and when the truth is finally free, her life is changed forever.

www.amazon.com

Finding Lucy

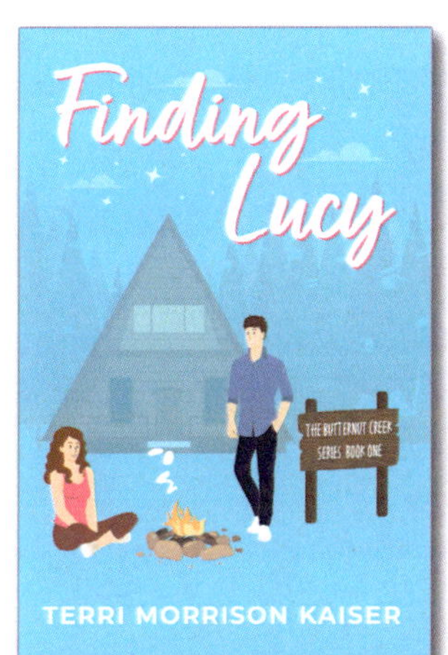

Moonlight Bay Camp saved Lucy and her sister in their youth. Big city developer Ian Flynn is threatening the future of the camp, and Lucy isn't about to stand still for it. What can a small-town girl do against big-city money and a big-city ego? Turns out, quite a lot. Only time and a terrifying accident will seal their fate.

www.amazon.com

Kissing Livvy

Lumberjack Jesse Tully's life is full to the brim with a disapproving father, a troubled teenager, his crabby grandma, and a struggling family business. The last thing he needed was to find Livvy Sherman, an environmental protester, dumped on his doorstep. Funny thing is, with no family of her own, Livvy gives Jesse and his family what they need most. But Livvy has never remained anywhere for long. The open road is looking mighty tempting.

www.amazon.com

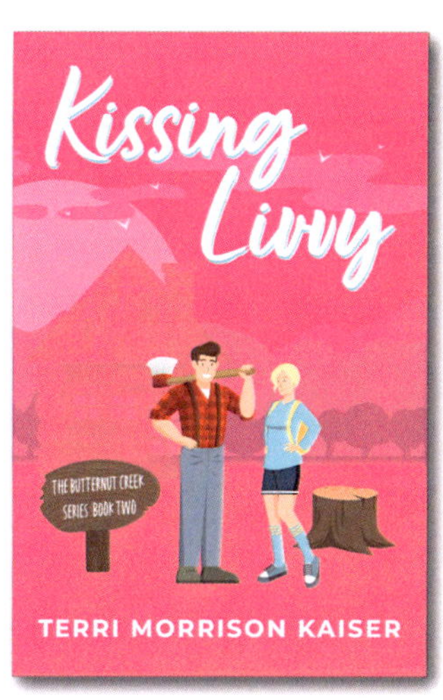

Ann Peck

Ann Peck is the award-winning author of Smiling on the Outside: Secrets, Sex, Shame and the Search for Self-Love. An adoptee and storyteller, she continues to write on identity and belonging. Her voice—both vulnerable and strong—invites readers to seek connection and discover courage within their own untold stories.

https://iamannpeck.substack.com

Ask the Author

What inspired you to write your latest (or favorite) book? Smiling on the Outside came from a reckoning—the realization that the polished life I showed the world didn't match my inner truth. Writing gave me a way to survive, and then a way to connect. My hope was, and still is, that no one has to feel alone in their struggle.

What's a favorite line or passage from your book? What stays with me most isn't a single line but the heartbeat of my work: reminding readers you're not alone, you're not the only one, and you're not crazy either. That truth is woven through *Smiling on the Outside* and continues to guide everything I write.

Why do you write? I write because it's how I make sense of life. Words turn pain into meaning and isolation into connection. It allows me to give voice to what was once hidden—and to remind every reader: you are not alone, not the only one, and not crazy either.

What's one thing readers often don't know about your work? One thing readers don't always realize is that Smiling on the Outside is a collection of essays, woven together to tell a larger story.

What's next for you as an author? What's next for me is simple: to keep writing the truths that connect us.

In three words, describe your writing style. Honest. Vulnerable. Hopeful.

"Writing gave me a way to survive, and then a way to connect. "

Smiling on the Outside: Secrets, Sex, Shame and the Search for Self-Love

What happens when the life you've built no longer fits the person you've become?

In Smiling on the Outside, Ann Peck pulls back the curtain on her seemingly perfect world to reveal the struggles with shame, secrets, and self-worth hiding underneath. With honesty and humor, she takes readers on a journey through heartbreak, reinvention, and resilience, reminding us that the pursuit of self-love is never straightforward—but always worth it.

Part inspiration, part rallying cry, this award-winning book offers connection to anyone who has ever tried to hold it all together on the outside while breaking inside. Ann's story is both personal and universal, reminding us that even after years pass, its truth remains: healing is possible, courage is contagious, and new beginnings are always within reach.

www.amazon.com

Awards

Finalist – Self-Help: Relationships (American Legacy Book Awards, 2024)

Finalist – Women's Issues/Women's Studies (American Legacy Book Awards, 2024)

Finalist – Relationships (Next Generation Indie Book Awards, 2017)

Finalist – Self-Help: Relationships (International Book Awards, 2017)

Finalist – Self-Help: Relationships (American Book Fest Best Book Awards, 2017)

Finalist – Women's Issues (National Indie Excellence Awards, 2017)

Gold Medal – Sexuality/Femininity (Living Now Book Awards, 2017)

Winner – Sexuality (National Indie Excellence Awards, 2017)

Publisher's Weekly (BookLife) described Smiling on the Outside as a sincere, tell-all collection of vignettes in which Peck's openness and belief in helping others is admirable. With candor and courage, she invites readers into a journey of resilience and healing.

Carla Pritchett

Carla Pritchett is a writer, speaker, group facilitator, former hospice bereavement coordinator, and artist.

Carla's heart and passions are reflected in the quality of her relationships. She loves to travel, journal in coffee shops, study metaphysics and the healing arts and spend time in nature.

https://authorcarlapritchett.com

Ask the Author

What inspired you to write your latest (or favorite) book? My curiosity and desire to understand relationships at a deeper level led to the writing of this book.

What's one thing readers often don't know about your work? My book was 35 years in the making.

What's a favorite line or passage from your book? It's only when we can be true to ourselves within the context of a relationship that we can really give from the depths of our heart.

Why do you write? I write because I am inspired to share what is within me. I write because I believe we are here to learn and if we can embrace our learning the wisdom gained holds great value.

What's next for you as an author? Publication of a second book currently titled Connect to Your Soul in and Ever-Changing World.

In three words, describe your writing style. My writing style is intuitive, personal, and heart centered.

Awards

Gold Award Winner 2023,
Midwest Book Awards
MIPA

" I write because I am inspired to share what is within me."

Getting to the HEART of Relationships: The MAGIC of Relationships and Their Power to HEAL, a Guide to Creating Mutually Supportive and Loving Relationships

Relationships are opportunities to learn and grow. Often, that isn't how we approach them. Because of that, we are quickly disillusioned. We need to go deeper within ourselves to discover the real meaning of love. We think love is something someone else gives to us. We think love given to us is conditional, so we try to live our lives to please another. What if instead we learn to be true to ourselves and to give ourselves the love we think we need from another.

www.amazon.com

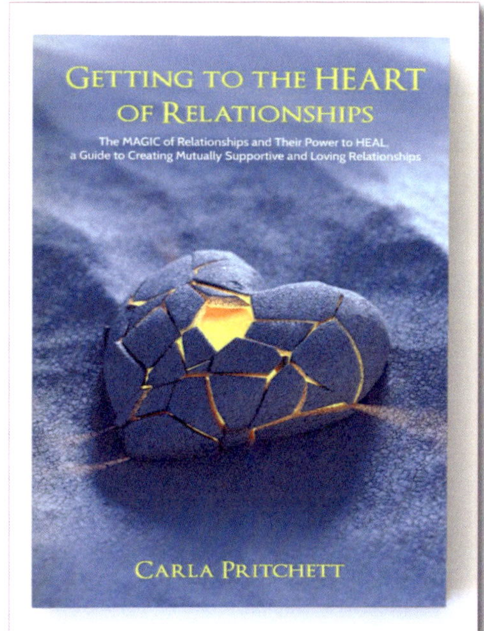

Excerpt

Being True to Yourself

Relationships are very complex. A great deal of love, pain, and joy is possible within a relationship between two people. What do you each want to bring to the other? You might say love and joy, but what do you bring to the other person in your relationship?

 Ask yourself:

• What does it mean to bring another person love and joy?

• Does it mean I have to be a perfect person?

• Does it mean I have to do everything exactly the way the other person want me to?

• What if I don't really know what the other person wants, and no matter what I do, it doesn't seem to be right?

• Do I then berate myself and try even harder to be the person I think I should be, or do I lovingly support myself and decide what I am going to do most of all is to be true to myself?

When you aren't being true to yourself, who are you being true to? Who do you think you are then? Are you someone anyone can trust? How can you trust a person who won't be honest with you about who they really are?

Sarah Routman

Sarah is a published poet, photographer, author, painter, and coloring book artist. She is a globally recognized Laughter Ambassador and Laughter Yoga instructor who loves to share the magic of art in its many forms, together with laughter and its many benefits to keep us functioning at our best.

www.LaughHealthy.com

Ask the Author

What inspired you to write your latest (or favorite) book? As I presented laughter sessions for people and trained other Laughter Yoga leaders, I was aware that people wanted to continue to practice laughing on their own for stress relief and overall wellness, but had a hard time remembering what to do or weren't feeling confident to do it on their own. I wanted to put something in people's hands that would empower them to create their own healthy laughter practice.

Why do you write? I write poetry to reveal to myself things that I might not otherwise want to deal with.

What's one thing readers often don't know about your work? I am a very independent and private person. Most of my creative endeavors are done alone.

What's a favorite line or passage from your book? By Irving Berlin: "Life is 10% what happens to you and 90% how you respond."

"I wanted to put something in people's hands that would empower them to create their own healthy laughter practice."

Discover the Power of Laughter: Jump-start your journey to health and joy

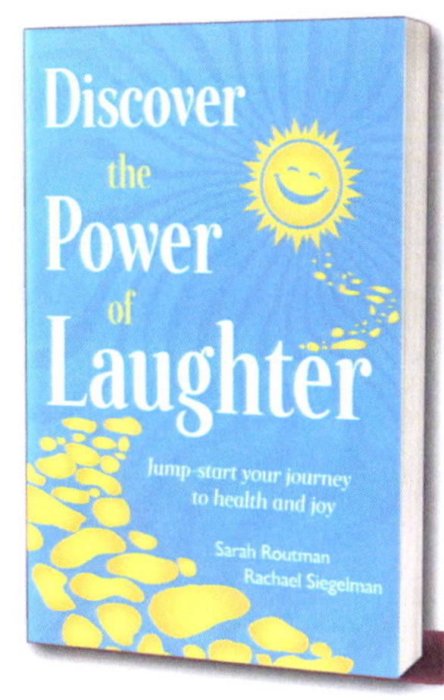

Discover the Power of Laughter explores the stories of identical twin authors. It takes the reader on a journey of self-discovery and reveals the superpower of laughter to influence all aspects of life.

Awaken childhood play, tap into the inner playground of laughter, and celebrate life's everyday moments for an unexpected boost to overall health and wellness.

www.DiscoverThePowerOfLaughter.com

Light Through Open Windows: Anniversary Edition

Light Through Open Windows is both an exploration of light and a collaboration of words and images. Looking back on her early work, Sarah reexamines the themes in both photographs and poems she wrote during college. As she reflects back, she discovers the parallels in familiar emotions that have traveled with her throughout the years.

www.amazon.com

Brushstrokes and Breaths: Meditation with Paint

Paint-Pouring Meets Photography. "When people ask me what equipment I use, I tell them my eyes."

What began as a paint-pouring experiment with a friend quickly became something more. I discovered that painting with my camera - capturing the ever-changing movement of paint - was just as compelling as the painting itself.

www.amazon.com

Mary Jane Schultz

Mary Jane Schultz often writes under the penname Leandra Logan. She is a best-selling, award-winning author published in numerous genres, including romance, mystery, young adult, and illustrated books for children. Recently, her manual for aspiring authors, Write Like Nobody's Watching, won a silver medal at MIPA's Midwest Book Awards.

Ask the Author

What inspired you to write your latest (or favorite) book? I wanted to share my knowledge with aspiring writers. I wrote the kind of manual I would have found useful years ago.

In three words, describe your writing style. Heartfelt, Humorous, Insightful

Why do you write? I was born to write. Even if I chose another career path, I would still be writing for fun.

What's one thing readers often don't know about your work? I write my first draft in longhand.

Awards

Silver medal at MIPA's Midwest Book Awards

Write Like Nobody's Watching: A Writers Manual

DO YOU HAVE A STORY TO TELL?

THERE IS ALWAYS ROOM FOR ONE MORE AUTHOR AT MJ'S WRITERS CAFÉ!

Storytelling is an exciting and rewarding adventure I encourage you to pursue.

The greatest challenge is translating your vision into a format others can understand and appreciate.

I have developed a step-by-step guide to help you properly construct a satisfying plot featuring lifelike characters from start to finish.

Come and explore your talent.

WRITE LIKE NOBODY'S WATCHING

www.amazon.com

" I was born to write. Even if I chose another career path, I would still be writing for fun. "

✦ Rachael Siegelman ✦

Rachael is an accomplished student of personal development; a lawyer, licensed mediator, certified Laughter Yoga leader, trained doula, childbirth educator, and infant massage instructor. She has trained thousands of medical professionals in Positive Patient Communication and continues to empower people to design and integrate laughter habits into their lives.

www.DiscoverThePowerOfLaughter.com

Ask the Author

What inspired you to write your latest (or favorite) book? My greatest joy is when I find opportunities to contribute to others. As Sarah started to develop her laughter keychain, we began to work together on it and it snowballed into a full collaboration resulting in this book

What's one thing readers often don't know about your work? It didn't come naturally for me to write a book. It came from years of work, layers of research, editing, adding layers, and continuous application and learning.

What's next for you as an author? In addition to creating several themed card decks to compliment Discover the Power of Laughter, I am working on a series of children's books based on the book.

What's a favorite line or passage from your book? I was in one of my funks. Sarah marched me to a mirror and forced me to look at our relections. Smiling into the mirror, she asked, "What do you see?"

"You're beautiful," I said.

"We're identical twin," she said. "We look exactly alike! If I'm beautiful, you are beautiful."

"But I'm ugly," I whispered.

"Don't you dare call me ugly!" Sarah said. She made silly faces until I started to giggle. Finally, when we were both laughing, Sarah said, "Now, don't you see, we're both beautiful?"

In three words, describe your writing style. Autobiographical. Insightful. Instructional.

Discover the Power of Laughter: Jump-start your journey to health and joy

Discover the Power of Laughter explores the stories of identical twin authors. It takes the reader on a journey of self-discovery and reveals the superpower of laughter to influence all aspects of life.

www.DiscoverThePowerOfLaughter.com

"I write to remember and I write to share."

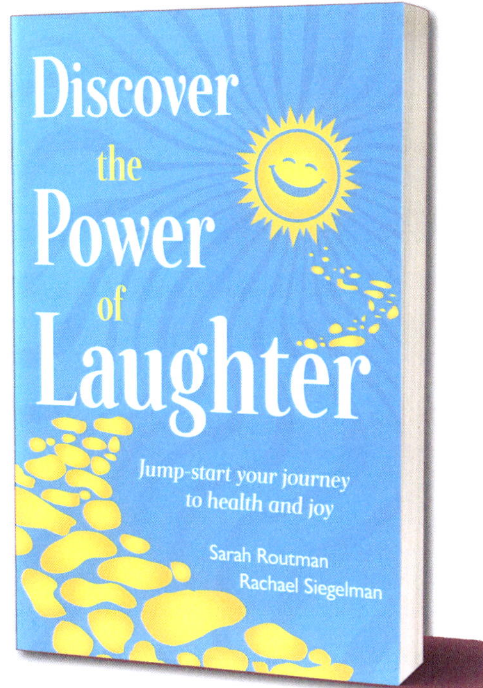

Excerpt

Whoa, do people actually laugh at themselves? Could I learn to laugh at myself?...

Laughing at myself seemed like a good idea. . . I was not going to mock myself!

How do I take myself and life less seriously and still keep everything under control?

Instead of becoming more light-hearted, I focused intensely on doing excellent schoolwork and becoming a leader in my youth group. I was a perfectionist. I was not going to laugh at myself—I saw that as cruel. Still, I wanted to be known for something, like Sarah [my joyous twin sister] was known as fun and spontaneous. Being identified as serious was fine with me until people mistook my intensity for unhappiness. . . .

In the intimate safe space of the Laughter Yoga training, my deep-seated inhibitions toward laughter began to melt away.... When we paused long enough to breathe [during a laughter dancing game] I noticed I was fully present and having fun. . . I was excited to re-discover my sense of play. I wondered if I would be able to let go like this again. . .

It's been more than nine years since [that game]. I can confirm, indeed, I can and did let go, again and again.

Mary Walerak

Mary Walerak holds a BA in Psychology and an MA in Human Development. With over 15 years as a life and health coach, she brings her passion for positive psychology into storytelling. In retirement, she crafted a magical tale of empowerment, first inspired as a loving guide for her grandchildren.

www.authormarywalerak.com

Ask the Author

What inspired you to write your latest (or favorite) book? Writing a book has always been a dream I have had. With retirement, the pandemic, and a little extra time on my hands, I wanted to write something that I could leave as a legacy for my grandchildren.

What's one thing readers often don't know about your work? I wanted this to be a story that will teach the reader some of life's important lessons in a way that is fun and will stay with them long after the book is read.

"I love the idea of creating something that is totally from my imagination."

Why do you write? I love the idea of creating something that is totally from my imagination.

What's next for you as an author? I am thinking of a trilogy of short stories that would further develop some of the characters from Alineade and develop more of the backstory about the Land of Alineade.

What's a favorite line or passage from your book? "There's always a do over." Friends that have read the book always seem to keep repeating it to me.

In three words, describe your writing style. Creative and imaginative, storytelling.

Finding Alineade

Finding Alineade invites readers into the curious tale of Charlie, a girl stepping from childhood into the maze of middle school. When whispers of a hidden realm appear at the edges of ordinary life, Charlie meets unusual friends, confronts a formidable nemesis, and discovers that magic often begins inside us. Guided by instinct and the quiet nudge of intuition, she learns to trust her abilities, face fears, and claim the person she's always dreamed of becoming. Adventure sparkles through every chapter—locker-room dramas, riddling creatures, impossible choices—and yet the story stays rooted in challenges every kid knows: belonging, courage, and staying true to yourself. Young readers will cheer for Charlie's heart and humor as she follows her own path and turns ordinary moments into extraordinary discoveries.

www.kirkhousepublishers.com/marywalerak

Description

Finding Alineade is the curious tale of a young girl named Charlie, who has left childhood behind and entered the confusing, sometimes intimidating world of middle school. Blending fantasy, a cast of unusual friends, and a formidable nemesis, the story follows Charlie as she discovers who she truly is. She learns to tap into the power within herself to become the person she has always dreamed of being. By trusting her instincts, believing in her abilities, and listening to that quiet nudge of intuition, she finds the courage to follow her own unique path.

Young readers will love this book for its sense of adventure, relatable challenges, and the magical world that feels both exciting and inspiring. Charlie's journey shows that even the most ordinary moments can lead to extraordinary discoveries.

Wouldn't it be wonderful if we could all step into the magical world of Alineade? Maybe, in some way, we can.

✦ Allison Amy Wedell ✦

Allison Amy Wedell (formerly Schumacher) is the author of Shaking Hands with Shakespeare: A Teenager's Guide to Reading and Performing the Bard. Her work has been published on MomsRising.org, BabyCenter.com, TheManifestStation.net, and her own blog, TeamEricChronicles. com. She writes about such diverse subjects as child sexual abuse prevention, parenting, and grief.

www.facebook.com/AllisontheWordsmith

Ask the Author

What inspired you to write your latest (or favorite) book? Sometime during the year 2000, my mom sent me—a professional actor at the time and giant Shakespeare fan with two theater degrees and one English degree—an article from the Smithsonian Magazine about how American settlers, traders, and mountain men in the Old West would entertain one another with vast swaths of memorized Shakespeare or welcome traveling troupes performing full-length plays in rough, informal settings.

Why do you write? I write to tell stories, to teach and inform.

What's a favorite line or passage from your book? "...people often lump Shakespearean theatre into the same groups as the ballet or the opera—elitist pastimes rather than popular entertainment. If Shakespeare saw us treating his plays this way, he would probably laugh. His plays were never meant to be lofty or snooty or exclusive or even very sophisticated—and they shouldn't be today, either. There are even fart jokes in Shakespeare. When was the last time you heard about a fart joke in a ballet?

In three words, describe your writing style. conversational, humorous, immediate

"I couldn't get the image out of my mind. Cowboys? Reciting Shakespeare?"

Shaking Hands with Shakespeare: A Teenager's Guide to Reading and Performing the Bard

Most people's first introduction to Shakespeare is as a "book" in high school English class. But plays aren't books, so why stick your nose in a book when the Bard should be three-dimensional?

Put your nose in this one, instead. It's an overview of Shakespeare's work with a heavy emphasis on acting and getting involved in the material. You'll learn about Shakespeare's life, the times he lived in, and how to understand his language.

www.abebooks.com

Excerpt

What?

Okay, I'll admit it: Shakespeare is hard. Hard to read, hard to understand. Few people in the world can sit down and read Shakespeare as if it were the Sunday comics. The rest of us, myself included, find reading Shakespeare to be a bit of a struggle—an extremely rewarding struggle, but a struggle nonetheless.

Although Shakespeare's language is very beautiful, it can be difficult to understand. Anybody from the 21st century can still relate to Shakespeare's characters and to the situations they find themselves in; it's just that they speak so differently than we do today.

But if language is the only barrier we have to cross, we can overcome that in no time. By "overcome that," I mean you'll be speaking Shakespeare's language soon. After all, the purpose of this book isn't to have more people sitting in rooms by themselves reading Shakespeare silently. The reason for that may surprise you: Shakespeare's plays were never meant to be read.

Huh?! I'll say it again:

SHAKESPEARE'S PLAYS WERE NEVER MEANT TO BE READ.

They were meant to be heard. They were meant to be seen. They were meant to be acted.

Cole W. Williams

Cole W. Williams is a poet, essayist, and hybrid writer. Select work are featured in The Common, Water~Stone Review, North Dakota Quarterly, and Flyway. Williams was recognized by The Florida Review's Humboldt Prize for "Sunset" and the International Human Rights Arts Festival: Creators of Justice Award for "The Godwin Essay."

www.amazon.com/stores/Cole-W.-Williams

Ask the Author

What inspired you to write your latest (or favorite) book? The 70's and 80's! Love those eras.

What's one thing readers often don't know about your work? I aspire to write a play in the future.

What's a favorite line or passage from your book? I do love the ending of Olympia.

Why do you write? It just spills out of me, my hard-drive, phone and desktop are a mess. It won't leave me alone.

What's next for you as an author? I will be looking to publish another book, and working on one more book after that; and then a play.

In three words, describe your writing style. Spontaneous. Raw. Uncut.

Awards

the Under Review second annual chapbook contest winner.

"It just spills out of me, my hard-drive, phone and desktop are a mess. It won't leave me alone."

Unfurl: a poetry reader

Unfurl is a tour of inspired poems. Musings from great writers, nature, northern boarders, and on writing. Light and approachable. Great for beginning poets.

www.amazon.com

Olympia

Winner of the second annual the Under Review chapbook contest. Olympia is an ekphrastic prose piece on the body as form, inspired by the docudrama The Pump featuring Arnold and Lou.

www.underreviewlit.com/shop/

✦ **Mary Jo Wiseman, CMP** ✦

Certified Meeting Professional, Mary Jo (MJ) Wiseman, spent 24 years in the meeting and hospitality industry as a corporate meeting planner where she managed the full spectrum of the event planning process across all levels of management with an emphasis on high profile, executive level groups including their Board of Directors, senior management and key customers (agents and brokers.)

Ask the Author

What inspired you to write your latest (or favorite) book? Planning successful meetings requires a lot of time and attention to detail. It is a process that is developed over time. It takes practice. It takes patience. And it takes making mistakes along the way which in the end will make you better, stronger and wiser. I wanted to share what I learned along the way with others to help them learn and grow and perhaps eliminate some unnecessary mishaps along the way.

"And it takes making mistakes along the way which in the end will make you better, stronger and wiser."

What's a favorite line or passage from your book? Never stop learning.

Why do you write? To teach, to encourage, to help others want to learn and do better.

In three words, describe your writing style. It's me.

What's one thing readers often don't know about your work? As a meeting planner, one would assume that I had "planned" to be a meeting planner all along. That was not at all the case. My goal in life early on was to simply be a wife and mother — but in terms of having a career plan of sorts, that was not in my "plan." I actually "fell into" my role as a meeting planner and that didn't happen until I was believe it or not just under the age of 40.

The Meeting Planning Process: A Guide to Planning Successful Meetings

"The Meeting Planning Process: A Guide to Planning Successful Meetings" offers a commonsense approach to managing the meeting planning process based on the knowledge and experience the author acquired during her career as a corporate meeting planner.

She shares her secrets for success throughout this book on how her approach to project management helped her to get and stay focused on the task at hand while handling multiple details, projects and deadlines. Whether you are a novice planner or an administrative professional who has been called upon to plan a meeting over and above your normal day-to-day responsibilities, this Guide will help bring ORDER to the planning process.

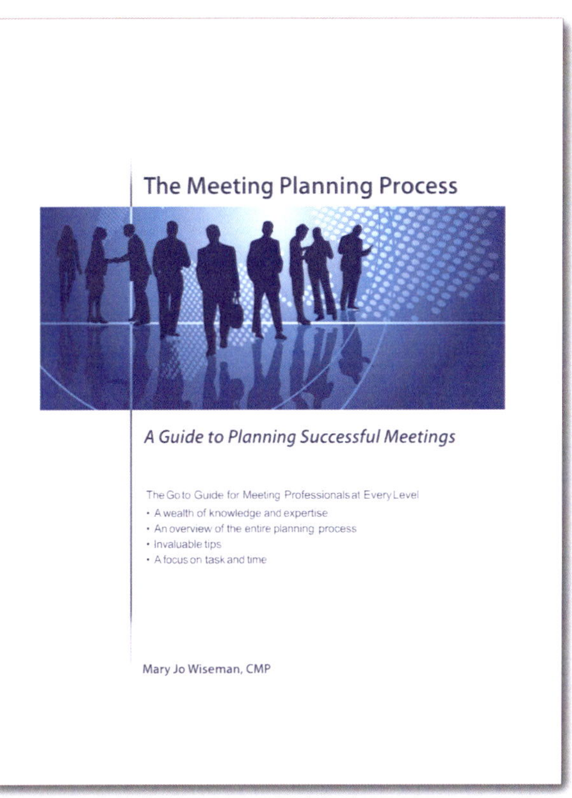

www.amazon.com

Excerpt

"A meeting planner by MY definition is the go-to person and would/should be a key member of the design (or planning) team with an organization — be it corporate, association or otherwise — charged with the responsibility of planning and executing a meeting or special event.

Planners utilize their project management experience, planning skills and attention to details to help create and deliver events that meet or exceed expectations. They add value to an organization by drawing upon their knowledge of the hospitality industry to manage expense and minimize risk by negotiation the best all-around rates and paying attention to contract terms.

A meeting planner has the keen ability to bring the right people and resources together to create and deliver ...."

The Sound of Her Story

"We are the descendants of the wild women you forgot… because it takes a single wild ember to bring a whole wildfire to life."

— *Wild Embers*, lyrics by Nikita Gill

Discovering a new voice that speaks directly to you is a magical moment. Written or sung, alone or in a crowd, this voice can impart joy, understanding, discovery, sorrow, healing, knowledge, or inspiration. Each voice has power, a power it shares with every reader, every listener, every person who pauses to hear it.

Perhaps it's a line in a novel that captures exactly what you've been feeling. Or the swell of harmony in a concert hall that makes your breath catch. Or a passage that opens a door to a world you've never considered.

Within these pages, you'll meet women authors whose words carry the full spectrum of human experience. Each writer offers her unique voice, her distinct perspective, and her personal truth. We hope among these voices, you will find one which resonates deeply with you.

AMPLIFYING WOMEN'S VOICES TOGETHER

Three of the authors in this book are also members of the Twin Cities Women's Choir. They express themselves through written word and through song. Their dual artistry reminded us women's voices take many forms, and all deserve to be celebrated. It also introduced us to an organization which shares our purpose to amplify women's voices.

For twenty-seven years, the Twin Cities Women's Choir has been creating space for women's voices to be heard. With 140 singers ranging from age 19 to 89, they gather weekly to breathe, listen, and tell stories through music, movement, and harmony. All are welcome. The choir provides a safe haven which includes teachers, scientists, artists, mothers, daughters, and grandmothers. Together they form a living archive of women's stories—resilient, wise, and beautifully diverse.

Twin Cities Women's Choir is non-auditioned because they believe everyone has a voice worth hearing. There is no gatekeeping. They achieve musical excellence through lifting each other up with collaboration, hard work, and joy.

Their artistic director, Randi Grundahl Rexroth, approaches each concert with the care of a storyteller. Every performance begins with a theme, a central thread that guides the selection of pieces and creates a narrative arc. Like a well-crafted book, a well-planned concert seeks to take you on a journey.

They want to make you feel, to leave you changed by the experience. Each piece is chosen to honor women's stories and build toward a powerful collective experience.

Whether part of a performance, or simply during rehearsal, the choir's songs become a mirror of their shared lives. They've sung A Meditation on Breathing after a profound local tragedy, celebrated milestones with weekly birthday songs, and lifted each other through loss and joy alike. One member captured it best: "Our artistic director gives us lessons in music and in life."

YOUR INVITATION

This book is more than a collection of author profiles and excerpts. It's an invitation to discovery—to explore new voices, to find stories that speak to your

Artist Dessa visits with the choir to share the message behind her lyrics for Controlled Burn.

soul, and perhaps to encounter your next favorite woman author.

The authors featured here have done the hard work of crafting their stories. The Twin Cities Women's Choir has done the hard work of building a community where every voice matters. Now it's your turn to discover which voices will become part of your life's soundtrack.

When women's voices—whether in song or on the page—are given space to be heard, something shifts. In the room. In the audience. In us.

Welcome to your next discovery.

Learn more about the Twin Cities Women's Choir at hervoiceproductions. org, including upcoming concerts.

Where Voices Become Family

The Twin Cities Women's Choir is more than a choir — it's a community.

We show up for one another in celebration and in sorrow, through laughter and through tears.

When one of our choir sisters left rehearsal early because she'd be getting married that weekend, we broke into "Going to the Chapel" as she walked out the door — a joyful, spontaneous send-off filled with harmony and laughter.

And when tragedy struck nearby Annunciation School, we arrived at rehearsal heavy with emotion — grieving for the families whose loved ones were lost or injured. Everyone said the same thing...they were tempted to stay home on the couch, but they knew coming was important...that it would be better. That night, our director didn't rush us into warm-ups. She acknowledged the weight in the room and quietly led us into the song Meditation on Breathing.

"Breathe in, breathe out.

When I breathe in, I breathe in peace.

When I breathe out, I breathe out love."

As our voices intertwined, tears came — but so did comfort. And that night, we left lighter.

This choir is filled with smart, thoughtful, kind, feeling women who are diverse in many ways, yet deeply connected.

Our leaders create space to be who we are and sing our way through whatever comes our way together.

Credit: A Choir Member

"TCWC is about women lifting women — one note, one breath, one song at a time."

Beyond the Page

Surprising Stories from Our Authors

Our featured writers lead lives as compelling as the stories they tell. From adventurers who've bungee-jumped in New Zealand and traveled to remote corners of the globe, to survivors who've faced down death and emerged stronger, to artists who express themselves through ballet, music, and reiki, these women will surprise you.

Resilient Survivors

Some of our authors have overcome profound challenges that forever changed their perspectives.

I've faced three near-death experiences, but recovered to tell my stories. Alexis Acker-Halbur

Something that's surprising about me is I survived 5 heart attacks and open-heart surgery. It was the most transformational thing that has happened to me. Katelyn Davida Mariah

At 64, I divorced and started over in a new town where I knew no one. Terri Morrison Kaiser

Unbounded Creativity

Creativity takes many forms, and these authors express themselves through multiple artistic disciplines.

I was once in a touring ballet company. Mary Walerak

I sing in the 130-voice women's choir, and blending in six-part harmony is one of the purest joys I know. Music, like leadership, is about listening, adapting, and finding rhythm together. And for contrast, I once bungy-jumped in New Zealand. I'm not a extreme risk taker, but I love mini-adventures. That leap still reminds me that fear and courage often travel together. Stacey Larsen, Ed.D.

As a patron of the GUTHRIE THEATER, I see many of the shows more than once! Mary K Crawford-Lorfink

Adventurers and World Travelers

These authors seek experiences beyond the familiar, venturing to remote destinations and embracing adventures that expand their understanding of the world and themselves.

I have my marine Captain's License now. Woot, All Aboard! Cole W. Williams

One of the reasons behind my new book is that I love to travel. Here's the part most people don't know. I tend to travel 'off the beaten path' more than to prestigious travel destinations. To list but a few, I've been to Trondheim Norway, Ganges River India, San Juan Comalapa Guatemala, and Galapagos islands Ecuador and probably the most remote place is where my husband and I were married, Idunda Tanzania. Leanne M. Benson

Service and Leadership

Whether through military service or civic leadership, these authors have dedicated themselves to serving their communities and making a difference.

I'm a veteran, who fulfilled a career in the Dutch military. I became a member of the Minnesota chapter of Warrior Writers—a nationwide nonprofit organization dedicated to helping veterans and active-duty service members express their experiences through creative writing and art. Dominique Miller

I was elected to be the mayor of the City of Savage in 2024. Being mayor is a very different career from being an author, but I love both. Each career allows me to make a small difference in this world. C. Kelley

Real Life Plot Twists

Life rarely follows a straight line, and these authors found themselves on journeys they never anticipated.

If someone had told me when I was younger, I would one day write a book about a career I ended up so thoroughly enjoying but never planned for, I would have thought them crazy. Mary Jo Wiseman, CMP

I am a reiki master. Carla Pritchett

I am fluent in German, and am ferociously learning Italian right now. I love languages! Early in my writing career, I carried a notebook with me and took notes every time something inspired me. I scribbled all these notes in GERMAN, because I was so afraid of people looking over my shoulder, reading all my notes, and stealing my ideas! Amy Gleason

I am dipping my toe into online dating!!! Oy! Katherine Barton

I am a wife, and mom in a blended family of 6 children, 3 of whom are mine and my husband's natural children. All six were home births. We are up to 12 grandchildren, (four born at home), and counting. Rachael Siegelman

Everyday Commitments

Sometimes the most surprising thing about a person is their dedication to the simple, daily practices that keep them grounded, healthy, and moving forward.

I try to walk 5 miles everyday! Colleen Baldrica

From the extraordinary to the everyday, from survival to service, from adventure to art, these women are shaped by the richness of their lived experiences. Each story they tell carries echoes of these moments, challenges, and joys.

Where the Magic Happens

Dream Writing Spaces

Popular culture loves to paint writers as brooding souls, hunched in dimly lit rooms, consuming vast quantities of coffee, while feverishly creating their latest novel. Is this truly where the magic happens for today's authors?

We asked writers featured in this collection to share their favorite writing spaces. From cozy home offices to dramatic natural settings, from communal creative spaces to sensory outdoor experiences, each author has discovered her own perfect environment.

Cozy Home Offices

For many writers, the ideal creative space is close to home. She has a personal sanctuary filled with meaningful objects, beloved companions, and windows to the world beyond.

I love to write in my office, surrounded by photos, memorabilia, and shelves of books. Mary Jane Schultz

In my office looking out my window. Colleen Baldrica

I love to write in the peaceful solitude of my cozy office surrounded by my eclectic treasures and memories. Carla Pritchett

In my home office with my two Maine Coon Cats. Donna M. Cramer

This is where the magic happens! My favorite place to write—my high-tech kitchen table! Armed with colorful pens, and a cat or two (usually napping on my notes), this cozy corner is where stories come to life. And when the words just won't cooperate? No problem. I simply push back my chair and dance around the kitchen until inspiration comes twirling back in. Barb Greenberg

Views of Nature

For these women inspiration comes from staying connected to the natural world.

My favorite place to write is anywhere I can see the water—whether it's the ocean, a lake, or the smaller pond I look out on now. Much of Smiling on the Outside was written with that view. Water reminds me to flow, while nature all around keeps me grounded and connected to something bigger. Ann Peck

Upstairs under the skylight with a giant pine tree for company. Katherine Barton

I love to write in my three-season porch at my bistro table looking at the pool and trees in my backyard. Andrea Easton

It's no dream! My art studio sits on top of a

bluff surrounded by a state hardwood forest with a small stream carving its way through the valley. Most of my creative ideas have come while hiking our land. Often, I hurry back from my walk, plop onto a chair in one of the lofts overlooking a great room with a massive 21-foot stone fireplace, and I begin to write or sketch. Leanne M. Benson

I love to write outside surrounded by my pretend zoo of animals. I truly enjoy sitting on the lounge chair with the sun hitting my face, my laptop propped up in my lap, chickens cluckin' around, my dog sniffing in all the scents and my cats roaming the yard looking for the next blade of grass to devour. All of the senses are alert in that moment. It is like I can smell the sun and taste the air. Jennifer Bierma

Community and Connection

Not all writers need solitude. For some, the perfect creative space is defined less by location and more by the presence of fellow writers who provide support, feedback, and camaraderie.

During my professional acting days, I was lucky enough to be in the cast of a musical with two brilliant women who became my 'writer grrrls.' While we all still lived in the Seattle area, we would go on annual writing retreats over President's Day weekend wherever we could get a place to stay: a cabin, a beach house, and once even a yurt. We are now scattered from sea to shining sea, but we still review and provide feedback on one another's work. So when I dream of leaving the world behind and really hunkering down on a piece, the 'where' wouldn't really matter, as long as I could be with those two writer women. Allison Amy Wedell

Dream Writing Spaces

Sometimes a writer's ideal space is aspirational, a vision of total creative immersion and free from worldly concerns.

I'd love to be location independent, writing in coffee shops and on beaches around the world. Nicole Fende

I'd love to have a place with a view of the sunrise, the sunset, and the moon, where I could lose myself in writing poetry, painting, and taking photographs. If I didn't have to worry about feeding myself and could be completely immersed in the creative processes without any attention to time, that would be beyond my wildest dreams. Sarah Routman

Whether practical or aspirational, indoor or outdoor, solitary or communal, each writer has her own perfect place. A space that allows the writer to be fully present, deeply connected to her work, and open to wherever her creativity might lead.

List of Authors

About Creatopia

Welcome to Creatopia®, where creativity flourishes and creative voices come together to brighten the world. Founded on the belief creativity should be valued, nurtured, and celebrated, Creatopia™ is building a vibrant community dedicated to supporting artists, creators, and creative-minded individuals in bringing their unique visions to life.

At its heart, Creatopia® exists to spark and encourage creativity in everyone. The community focuses on inspiring people to tap into their own creative potential while also showcasing carefully curated works from independent creators. This dual mission of encouraging personal creativity while celebrating the creative achievements of others makes Creatopia® a unique space in the creative landscape.

We invite you to join us at www.creatopia.studio.

"Creatopia® exists to spark and encourage creativity in everyone."

www.ingramcontent.com/pod-product-compliance
Lightning Source LLC
Chambersburg PA
CBRC101119300726
48981CB00013B/476